The BIG Book of Moods

*Wisdom quotes about human emotions
from Plato to Oprah*

2

The BIG Book of Moods
edited by Claire Davis

littlebigbooks@icloud.com

Table of Contents

Anger

"For every minute you are angry

you lose sixty seconds of happiness."

Ralph Waldo Emerson

"There are two things a person should never be angry at, what they can help, and what they cannot."

Plato

"When anger rises, think of the consequences."

Confucius

"Anger is as a stone cast into a wasp's nest."

Pope Paul VI

"The angry people are those people who are most afraid."

Dr. Robert Anthony

"Speak when you are angry and you will make the best speech you'll ever regret."

Laurence J. Peter

"I have a right to my anger, and I don't want anybody telling me I shouldn't be, that it's not nice to be, and that something's wrong with me because I get angry."

Maxine Waters

"You will not be punished for your anger, you will be punished by your anger."

Buddha

"The greatest remedy for anger is delay."

Seneca

"Anger is a wind which blows out the lamp of the mind."

Robert Ingersoll

"Expressing anger is really important."

Nancy Todd

"Anger is the only thing to put off until tomorrow."

Czech Proverb

"If you kick a stone in anger, you'll hurt your own foot."

Korean Proverb

"In anger we should refrain both from speech and action."

Pythagoras

"Whatever is begun in anger ends in shame."

Benjamin Franklin

"Man should forget his anger before he lies down to sleep."

Mahatma Gandhi

"The opposite of anger is not calmness, its empathy."

Mehmet Oz

"Anger is an expensive luxury in which only men of certain income can indulge."

George William Curtis

"The more anger towards the past you carry in your heart, the less capable you are of loving in the present."

Barbara de Angelis

"Anger is a great force. If you control it, it can be transmuted into a power which can move the whole world."

William Shenstone

"When you start suppressing feelings at an early age, it hurts you down the road. Full expression of anger and pain is very important."

Andrew Shue

"To rule one's anger is well, to prevent it is better."

Tryon Edwards

"There was never an angry man that thought his anger unjust."

Saint Francis de Sales

"Anger becomes limiting, restricting. You can't see through it. While anger is there, look at that, too. But after a while, you have to look at something else."

Thylias Moss

"Life is precious and there's not a lot of room for anger."

Fran Drescher

Anxiety

"Anxiety is the space between
the "now" and the "then"."

Richard Abell

"I don't have big anxieties. I wish I did. I'd be much more interesting."

Roy Lichtenstein

"Anxiety is the dizziness of freedom."

Soren Kierkegaard

"You get rid of a certain anxiety by realizing you're not alone."

Olivia Mellan

"The act of birth is the first experience of anxiety, and thus the source and prototype of the affect of anxiety."

Sigmund Freud

"Anxiety is a good thing in some situations."

Mary Morrison

"Anxiety is the hand maiden of creativity."

T. S. Eliot

"Anxiety does not empty tomorrow of its sorrows, but only empties today of its strength."

Charles Spurgeon

"Our Age of Anxiety is, in great part, the result of trying to do today's job with yesterday's tools and yesterday's concepts."

Marshall McLuhan

"The natural role of twentieth-century man is anxiety."

Norman Mailer

"What else does anxiety about the future bring you but sorrow upon sorrow?"

Thomas Kempis

"I try not to worry about the future, so I take each day just one anxiety attack at a time."

Tom Wilson

"We are living in a new age of energy supply anxiety."

Daniel Yergin

"Concentration is a fine antidote to anxiety."

Jack Nicklaus

"When you get over the anxiety, you discover you should have been mad a long time ago."

Amy Clampitt

"The source of anxiety lies in the future. If you can keep the future out of mind, you can forget your worries."

Milan Kundera

Apathy

"Apathy is the glove into which
evil slips its hand."

Bodie Thoene

"Apathy is a sort of living oblivion."

Horace Greeley

"I have a very strong feeling that the opposite of love is not hate, it's apathy. It's not giving a damn."

Leo Buscaglia

"Apathy can be overcome by enthusiasm, and enthusiasm can only be aroused by two things: first, an ideal, with takes the imagination by storm, and second, a definite intelligible plan for carrying that ideal into practice."

Arnold J. Toynbee

"We may have found a cure for most evils, but we have found no remedy for the worst of them all: the apathy of human beings."

Helen Keller

"In communications, familiarity breeds apathy."

William Bernbach

"By far the most dangerous foe we have to fight is apathy, indifference from whatever cause, not from a lack of knowledge, but from carelessness, from absorption in other pursuits, from a contempt bred of self satisfaction."

William Osler

"Some people confuse acceptance with apathy, but there's all the difference in the world. Apathy fails to distinguish between what can and what cannot be helped; acceptance makes that distinction. Apathy paralyzes the will-to-action; acceptance frees it by relieving it of impossible burdens."

Arthur Gordon

"Apathy is a disease and some days I long for it."

Zoe Trope

Boredom

""I am bored" generally means "I am boring"."

Dennis Prager

"A healthy male adult bore consumes each year one and a half times his own weight in other people's patience."

John Updike

"He who seeks rest finds boredom. He who seeks work finds rest."

Dylan Thomas

"Is boredom anything less than the sense of one's faculties slowly dying?"

Sir Arthur Helps

"Someone's boring me. I think it's me."

Dylan Thomas

"There's no excuse to be bored. Sad, yes. Angry, yes. Depressed, yes. Crazy, yes. But there's no excuse for boredom, ever."

Viggo Mortensen

"The penalty for success is to be bored by the people who used to snub you."

Nancy Astor

"A bore is a man who, when you ask him how he is, tells you."

Bert Leston Taylor

"Boredom, after all, is a form of criticism. "

William Phillips

"Boredom is an emptiness filled with insistence."

Leo Stein

"Perhaps the world's second-worst crime is boredom; the first is being a bore."

Cecil Beaton

"Boredom is a big factor. When it's just a job, it's time to leave."

Dory Hollander

"One must choose in life between boredom and suffering."

Madame de Stael

"Boredom is always counter-revolutionary. Always."

Guy Debord

"Boredom is a self-inflicted insult."

Bill Purdin

"The life of the creative man is lead, directed and controlled by boredom. Avoiding boredom is one of our most important purposes."

Susan Sontag

"Boredom is the root of all evil, the despairing refusal to be oneself."

Soren Kierkegaard

"Boredom is a vital problem for the moralist, since half the sins of mankind are caused by the fear of it."

Bertrand Russell

"Isn't history ultimately the result of our fear of boredom?"

Emile M. Cioran

"Boredom: the desire for desires."

Leo Tolstoy

"The two enemies of human happiness are pain and boredom."

Arthur Schopenhauer

"In order to live free and happily you must sacrifice boredom. It is not always an easy sacrifice."

Richard Bach

"For boredom speaks the language of time, and it is to teach you the most valuable lesson of your life: the lesson of your utter insignificance."

Joseph Brodsky

"It's the boredom that kills you. You read until you're tired of that. You do crossword puzzles until you're tired of that. This is torture. This is mental torture."

Jack Kevorkian

"Boredom is just the reverse side of fascination: both depend on being outside rather than inside a situation, and one leads to the other."

Arthur Schopenhauer

"Nature is unfair? So much the better, inequality is the only bearable thing, the monotony of equality can only lead us to boredom."

Francis Picabia

"You'll find boredom where there is the absence of a good idea."

Earl Nightingale

Compassion

"If you want others to be happy,
practice compassion.
If you want to be happy,
practice compassion."

The Dalai Lama

"Compassion is not weakness, and concern for the unfortunate is not socialism."

Hubert H. Humphrey

"Compassion is a two way street."

Frank Capra

"By compassion we make others' misery our own, and so, by relieving them, we relieve ourselves also."

Thomas Browne, Sr.

"Compassion is the basis of all morality."

Arthur Schopenhauer

"If your compassion does not include yourself, it is incomplete."

Jack Kornfield

"Compassion is not a popular virtue."

Karen Armstrong

"Until he extends his circle of compassion to include all living things, man will not himself find peace."

Albert Schweitzer

"It's compassion that makes gods of us."

Dorothy Gilman

"Love and compassion are necessities, not luxuries. Without them humanity cannot survive."

Dalai Lama

"Compassion is sometimes the fatal capacity for feeling what it is like to live inside somebody else's skin. It is the knowledge that there can never really be any peace and joy for me until there is peace and joy finally for you too."

Frederick Buechner

"Compassion is the antitoxin of the soul: where there is compassion even the most poisonous impulses remain relatively harmless."

Eric Hoffer

"Compassion is a call, a demand of nature, to relieve the unhappy as hunger is a natural call for food."

Joseph Butler

"Skip the religion and politics, head straight to the compassion. Everything else is a distraction."

Talib Kweli

"Make no judgements where you have no compassion."

Anne McCaffrey

"Compassion brings us to a stop, and for a moment we rise above ourselves."

Mason Cooley

Depression

"Depression is when you have lots of love,
but no one's taking."

Douglas Coupland

"You largely constructed your depression. It wasn't given to you. Therefore, you can deconstruct it."

Albert Ellis

"Concern should drive us into action and not into a depression. No man is free who cannot control himself."

Pythagoras

"Depression is unfocused self-pity."

Bill Wilson

"Depression is the inability to construct a future."

Dr. Rollo May

"A lot of people don't realize that depression is an illness. I don't wish it on anyone, but if they would know how it feels, I swear they would think twice before they just shrug it."

Jonathan Davis

"That's the thing about depression: A human being can survive almost anything, as long as she sees the end in sight. But depression is so insidious, and it compounds daily, that it's impossible to ever see the end. The fog is like a cage without a key."

Elizabeth Wurtzel

"Depression occurs when one looks back with no pride, and looks forward with no hope."

Robert Frost

"Depression is melancholy minus its charms, the animation, the fits."

Susan Sontag

"Instead of seeing depression as a dysfunction, it is a functioning phenomenon. It stops you cold, sets you down, makes you damn miserable."

James Hillman

"Depression is something that makes you lose your sight."

Michael Schenker

"Depression scares people off. It makes me laugh that it has that kind of effect."

Siobhan Fahey

"I don't think anybody's continually happy, uh, except idiots, you know. You know, you have to have little moments of depression."

Rube Goldberg

Doubt

"He who knows nothing,
doubts nothing."

Spanish Proverb

"Doubt is the father of invention."

Galileo Galilei

"Our doubts are traitors, And make us lose the good we oft might win By fearing to attempt."

William Shakespeare

"If you would be a real seeker after truth, it is necessary that at least once in your life you doubt, as far as possible, all things."

Rene Descartes

"Beliefs are what divide people. Doubt unites them."

Peter Ustinov

"Doubt whom you will, but never yourself."

Christine Bovee

"I never could tell a lie that anybody would doubt, nor a truth that anybody would believe."

Mark Twain

"When in doubt, observe and ask questions. When certain, observe at length and ask many more questions."

George S. Patton

"The trouble with the world is that the stupid are cocksure and the intelligent are full of doubt."

Bertrand Russell

"Doubt is a pain too lonely to know that faith is his twin brother."

Khalil Gibran

"Doubt is part of all religion. All the religious thinkers were doubters."

Isaac Bashevis Singer

"The greater the artist, the greater the doubt. Perfect confidence is granted to the less talented as a consolation prize."

Robert Hughes

"Doubt, of whatever kind, can be ended by action alone."

Thomas Carlyle

"A fanatic is a man who consciously over compensates a secret doubt."

Aldous Huxley

"In doubt, fear is the worst of prophets."

Caecilius Statius

Fear

"The only thing to fear is fear itself."

Franklin D. Roosevelt

"There is great beauty in going through life without anxiety or fear. Half our fears are baseless, and the other half discreditable."

Christian Nestell Bovee

"Fear is the lengthened shadow of ignorance."

Arnold H. Glasgow

"There are times when fear is good. It must keep its watchful place at the heart's controls. There is advantage in the wisdom won from pain."

Aeschylus

"Men are moved by two levers only: fear and self interest."

Napoleon Bonaparte

"To overcome a fear, here's all you have to do: realize the fear is there, and do the action you fear anyway."

Peter McWilliams

"We fear the thing we want the most."

Dr. Robert Anthony

"Fear is a disease that eats away at logic and makes man inhuman."

Marian Anderson

"Curiosity will conquer fear even more than bravery will."

James Stephens

"Many of our fears are tissue paper-thin, and a single courageous step would carry us through them."

Brendan Francis

"Fear does not have any special power unless you empower it by submitting to it."

Les Brown

"Fear was the first thing on earth to make gods."

Lucretius

"Even the fear of death is nothing compared to the fear of not having lived authentically and fully."

Frances Moore Lappe

"Fear is the highest fence."

Dudley Nichols

"The constant assertion of belief is an indication of fear."

Jiddu Krishnamurti

"We fear things in proportion to our ignorance of them."

Christian Nevell Bovee

"There are very few monsters who warrant the fear we have of them."

Andre Gide

"Whatever you fear most has no power. It is your fear that has the power."

Oprah Winfrey

"You can conquer almost any fear if you will only make up your mind to do so. For remember, fear doesn't exist anywhere except in the mind."

Dale Carnegie

"Fear of a name increases fear of the thing itself."

J. K. Rowling

"Peace is that state in which fear of any kind is unknown."

John Buchan

"It's the most unhappy people who most fear change. "

Mignon McLaughlin

"Expose yourself to your deepest fear; after that, fear has no power, and the fear of freedom shrinks and vanishes. You are free."

Jim Morrison

"I learned that courage was not the absence of fear, but the triumph over it. The brave man is not he who does not feel afraid, but he who conquers that fear."

Nelson Mandela

"Nothing in life is to be feared, it is only to be understood."

Marie Curie

"To conquer fear is the beginning of wisdom."

Bertrand Russell

Gratitude

"Gratitude is when memory is stored
in the heart and not in the mind."

Lionel Hampton

"Gratitude is not only the greatest of virtues, but the parent of all others."

Cicero

"Feeling gratitude and not expressing it is like wrapping a present and not giving it."

William Arthur Ward

"No one who achieves success does so without acknowledging the help of others. The wise and confident acknowledge this help with gratitude."

Alfred North Whitehead

"To the generous mind the heaviest debt is that of gratitude, when it is not in our power to repay it."

Benjamin Franklin

"Silent gratitude isn't very much use to anyone."

Gertrude Stein

"The debt of gratitude we owe our mother and father goes forward, not backward. What we owe our parents is the bill presented to us by our children."

Nancy Friday

"Happiness is itself a kind of gratitude."

Joseph Wood Krutch

"Gratitude is one of those things that cannot be bought. It must be born with men, or else all the obligations in the world will not create it."

Edward F. Halifax

"Gratitude helps you to grow and expand; gratitude brings joy and laughter into your life and into the lives of all those around you."

Eileen Caddy

"Gratitude is a duty which ought to be paid, but which none have a right to expect."

Jean Jacques Rousseau

""Thank you" is the best prayer that anyone could say. I say that one a lot. Thank you expresses extreme gratitude, humility, understanding."

Alice Walker

"Gratitude makes sense of our past, brings peace for today, and creates a vision for tomorrow."

Melody Beattie

"Revenge is profitable, gratitude is expensive."

Edward Gibbon

Grief

"Grief is the price we pay for love."

Queen Elizabeth II

"Grief is a process, not a state."
Anne Grant

"The only cure for grief is action."
George Henry Lewes

"Grief teaches the steadiest minds to waver."
Sophocles

"Grief drives men into habits of serious reflection, sharpens the understanding, and softens the heart."
John Adams

"Tearless grief bleeds inwardly."
Christian Nevell Bovee

"While grief is fresh, every attempt to divert only irritates. You must wait till it be digested, and then amusement will dissipate the remains of it."
Samuel Johnson

"Waste not fresh tears over old griefs."
Euripides

"To spare oneself from grief at all cost can be achieved only at the price of total detachment, which excludes the ability to experience happiness."

Erich Fromm

"f we could not forget, we would never be free from grief."

Bahya Ibn Paquda

"Tears are the silent language of grief."

Voltaire

"Joy comes, grief goes, we know not how."

James Russell Lowell

"Happiness is beneficial for the body, but it is grief that develops the powers of the mind."

Marcel Proust

"Grief can't be shared. Everyone carries it alone. His own burden in his own way."

Anne Morrow Lindbergh

"Given a choice between grief and nothing, I'd choose grief."

William Faulkner

"If you suppress grief too much, it can well redouble."

Moliere

"You don't go around grieving all the time, but the grief is still there and always will be."

Nigella Lawson

"To touch a sore is to renew one's grief."

Terence

"Grief is a normal and natural response to loss. It is originally an unlearned feeling process. Keeping grief inside increases your pain."

Anne Grant

"One joy shatters a hundred griefs."

Chinese Proverb

"There is no grief like the grief that does not speak."

Henry Wadsworth Longfellow

"Grief makes one hour ten."

William Shakespeare

"In youth one has tears without grief; in age, griefs without tears."

Joseph Roux

"Grief is itself a medicine."

William Cowper

"To bury grief, plant a seed."

German Proverb

Guilt

"Guilt is the price we pay willingly
for doing what we are going to do anyway."

Isabelle Holland

"Guilt is anger directed at ourselves, at what we did or did not do."

Peter McWilliams

"Guilt is the very nerve of sorrow."

Horace Bushnell

"Guilt is a rope that wears thin."

Ayn Rand

"I'm an Irish Catholic and I have a long iceberg of guilt."

Edna O'brien

"I don't feel guilt. Whatever I wish to do, I do."

Jeanne Moreau

"Fear is the tax that conscience pays to guilt."

George Sewell

"Guilt is a supreme waste of time and energy."

Emily Giffin

Happiness

"Happiness is a mystery. Like religion."

G. K. Chesterton

"Happiness is not a goal, it is a by-product."
Eleanor Roosevelt

"Most folks are about as happy as they make up their minds to be."
Abraham Lincoln

"Happiness is a choice that requires effort at times."
Aeschylus

"Happiness makes up in height for what it lacks in length."
Robert Frost

"One of the keys to happiness is a bad memory."
Rita Mae Brown

"He who has no wish to be happier is the happiest of men."
William R. Alger

"You can't be envious and happy at the same time."
Frank Tyger

"It is pretty hard to tell what does bring happiness; poverty and wealth have both failed."

Kin Hubbard

"Objects we ardently pursue bring little happiness when gained; most of our pleasures come from unexpected sources."

Herbert Spencer

"No man is happy who does not think himself so."

Publilius Syrus

"The greatest happiness is to transform one's feelings into action."

Madame de Stael

"Happiness isn't something you experience, it's something you remember."

Oscar Levant

"All happiness or unhappiness solely depends upon the quality of the object to which we are attached by love."

Baruch Spinoza

"The secret of happiness is to admire without desiring."

Carl Sandburg

"The foolish man seeks happiness in the distance, the wise grows it under his feet."

James Oppenheim

"If we only wanted to be happy, it would be easy; but we want to be happier than other people, and that is almost always difficult, since we think them happier than they are."

Charles de Montesquieu

"The pursuit of happiness is a most ridiculous phrase: if you pursue happiness you'll never find it."

Carrie P. Snow

"Remember that the happiest people are not those getting more, but those giving more."

H. Jackson Brown, Jr.

"Remember that happiness is a way of travel, not a destination."

Roy M. Goodman

"No man is happy. He is, at best, fortunate."

Solon

"To be stupid, selfish, and have good health are three requirements for happiness, though if stupidity is lacking, all is lost."

Gustave Flaubert

"Money can't buy happiness, but it can make you awfully comfortable while you're being miserable."

Clare Boothe Luce

"A person is never happy except at the price of some ignorance."

Anatole France

"Whenever I get happy, I always have a terrible feeling."

Roman Polanski

"Happiness is when what you think, what you say, and what you do are in harmony."

Mahatma Gandhi

"It is not how much we have, but how much we enjoy, that makes happiness."

Charles Spurgeon

"Just do what must be done. This may not be happiness, but it is greatness."

George Bernard Shaw

"Desire is individual. Happiness is common."

Julian Casablancas

"Happiness is having a scratch for every itch."

Ogden Nash

"The first recipe for happiness is: Avoid too lengthy meditation on the past."

Andre Maurois

"To attain happiness in another world we need only to believe something, while to secure it in this world we must do something."

Charlotte Perkins Gilman

"The secret to happiness is to face the fact that the world is horrible."

Bertrand Russell

"Happiness is a butterfly, which when pursued, is always just beyond your grasp, but which, if you will sit down quietly, may alight upon you"

Nathaniel Hawthorne

"I've learned that everyone wants to live on top of the mountain, but all the happiness and growth occurs while you're climbing it."

Andy Rooney

"If you want to be happy, be."

Leo Nikolaevich Tolstoy

Hate

"As long as you hate,
there will be people to hate."

George Harrison

"Fear leads to anger. Anger leads to hate. Hate leads to suffering."

Yoda

"When we don't know who to hate, we hate ourselves."

Chuck Palahniuk

"Hate cannot drive out hate: only love can do that."

Martin Luther King Jr.

"If you hate a person, you hate something in him that is part of yourself. What isn't part of ourselves doesn't disturb us."

Hermann Hesse

"The hatred of those who are near to us is the most violent."

Publius Cornelius Tacitus

"We hate some persons because we do not know them; and we will not know them because we hate them."

Charles Caleb Colton

"Hate is all a lie, there is no truth in hate."

Kathleen Norris

"Hate is too great a burden to bear. It injures the hater more than it injures the hated."

Coretta Scott King

"Hate the sin and love the sinner."

Mahatma Ghandi

"I shall allow no man to belittle my soul by making me hate him."

Booker T. Washington

"Don't do anything by half. If you love someone, love them with all your soul. When you hate someone, hate them until it hurts."

Henry Rollins

"I don't hate people, I just feel better when they aren't around."

Charles Bukowski

"I honestly think it is better to be a failure at something you love than to be a success at something you hate."

George Burns

"I am free of all prejudices. I hate every one equally."

W. C. Fields

"From the deepest desires often come the deadliest hate."

Socrates

"You either love or you hate. You live in the middle, you get nothing."

Charlie Sheen

"It is easy to hate and it is difficult to love. This is how the whole scheme of things works. All good things are difficult to achieve, and bad things are very easy to get."

Rene Descartes

"Nothing can be love or hated unless it is first known."

Leonardo da Vinci

"I have decided to stick with love. Hate is too great a burden to bear."

Martin Luther King, Jr.

Hope

"Hope is like a road in the country: there was never a road, but when many people walk on it, the road comes into existence."

Lyn Yutang

"Appetite, with an opinion of attaining, is called hope; the same, without such opinion, despair."

Thomas Hobbes

"Hope is a talent like any other."

Storm Jameson

"Hope begins in the dark, the stubborn hope that if you just show up and try to do the right thing, the dawn will come. You wait and watch and work: you don't give up."

Anne Lamott

"Never deprive someone of hope, it might be all they have."

H. Jackson Brown Jr.

"It is difficult to say what is impossible, for the dream of yesterday is the hope of today and the reality of tomorrow."

Robert H. Goddard

"Hoping means seeing that the outcome you want is possible, and then working for it."

Bernie Siegel

"Hope doesn't come from calculating whether the good news is winning out over the bad. It's simply a choice to take action."

Anna Lappe

"Hope is a good thing, maybe the best thing, and no good thing ever dies."

Stephen King

"What one hopes for is always better than what one has."

Ethiopian Proverb

"Hope is a good breakfast, but it is a bad supper."

Sir Francis Bacon

"I am prepared for the worst, but hope for the best."

Benjamin Disraeli

"When we have lost everything, including hope, life becomes a disgrace, and death a duty."

W. C. Fields

"A whole stack of memories never equal one little hope."

Charles M. Schulz

"There is no medicine like hope, no incentive so great, and no tonic so powerful as expectation of something tomorrow."

Orison Swett Marden

"Hope will never be silent."

Harvey Milk

"Where there is no vision, there is no hope."

George Washington Carver

"Hope never abandons you, you abandon it."

George Weinberg

"All human wisdom is summed up in two words: wait and hope."

Alexandre Dumas

"Hope is the cordial that keeps life from stagnating. "

Samuel Richardson

"Expecting something for nothing is the most popular form of hope."

Arnold H. Glasow

Loneliness

"Loneliness is a strange gift."

E. B. White

"The worst loneliness is not to be comfortable with yourself."

Mark Twain

"When everyone leaves you it's loneliness you feel, when you leave everyone else it's solitude."

Alfred Polgar

"People drain me, even the closest of friends, and I find loneliness to be the best state in the union to live in."

Margaret Cho

"To be alone is to be different, to be different is to be alone."

Suzanne Gordon

"Loneliness is the universal problem of rich people."

Joan Collins

"The most terrible poverty is loneliness and the feeling of being unloved."

Mother Teresa

"Loneliness is very important for the survival of our species. It contributes to our humanity."

John Cacioppo

"Language has created the word "loneliness" to express the pain of being alone. And it has created the word "solitude" to express the glory of being alone."

Paul Tillich

"Loneliness seems to have become the great American disease."

John Corry

"No one ever discovers the depths of his own loneliness."

Georges Bernanos

"f you are afraid of loneliness, do not marry."

Anton Chekhov

"Loneliness adds beauty to life. It puts a special burn on sunsets and makes night air smell better."

Henry Rollins

"Forget sex or politics or religion, loneliness is the subject that clears out a room."

Douglas Coupland

"Loneliness is proof that your innate search for connection is intact."

Martha Beck

"Loneliness is and always has been the central and inevitable experience of every man."

Thomas Wolfe

"Loneliness is the ultimate poverty."

Abigail Van Buren

"Loneliness is the poverty of self; solitude is the richness of self."

May Sarton

"The surest sign of age is loneliness."

Annie Dillard

"It is strange to be known so universally and yet to be so lonely."

Albert Einstein

"Solitude is the profoundest fact of the human condition. Man is the only being who knows he is alone."

Octavio Paz

"Being human is the most terrible loneliness in the universe."

A.A. Attanasio

Love

"The way to love anything
is to realize that it may be lost."

Gilbert K. Chesterton

"We love because it's the only true adventure."

Nikki Giovanni

"You know you're in love when you can't fall asleep because reality is finally better than your dreams."

Dr. Seuss

"The meeting of two personalities is like the contact of two chemical substances: if there is any reaction, both are transformed."

Carl Jung

"There is always some madness in love. But there is also always some reason in madness."

Friedrich Nietzsche

"Love is, above all else, the gift of oneself."

Jean Anouilh

"If you wished to be loved, love."

Seneca

"Love is something eternal; the aspect may change, but not the essence."

Vincent van Gogh

"To say 'I love you' one must first be able to say the 'I'."

Ayn Rand

"Love is so short, forgetting is so long."

Pablo Neruda

"Love is composed of a single soul inhabiting two bodies."

Aristotle

"What we have once enjoyed we can never lose. All that we love deeply becomes a part of us."

Helen Keller

"Love is like handing someone a gun, having them point it at your heart, and trusting them to never pull the trigger."

Michael Gardner

"Perhaps the feelings that we experience when we are in love represent a normal state. Being in love shows a person who he should be."

Anton Chekhov

"The opposite of love is not hate, it's indifference."

Elie Wiesel

"Love is a sacred reserve of energy; it is like the blood of spiritual evolution."

Teilhard De Chardin

"We come to love not by finding a perfect person, but by learning to see an imperfect person perfectly."

Sam Keen

"Being deeply loved by someone gives you strength, while loving someone deeply gives you courage."

Lao Tzu

"Immature love says: "I love you because I need you". Mature love says "I need you because I love you"."

Erich Fromm

"Love does not begin and end the way we seem to think it does. Love is a battle, love is a war; love is a growing up."

James A. Baldwin

"First love is only a little foolishness and a lot of curiosity."

George Bernard Shaw

"Love is like war: easy to begin but very hard to stop."

H. L. Mencken

"Love can sometimes be magic. But magic can sometimes... just be an illusion."

Javan

"Love is an irresistible desire to be irresistibly desired."

Robert Frost

"It is difficult to know at what moment love begins; it is less difficult to know that it has begun."

Henry Wadsworth Longfellow

"Love consists in this, that two solitudes protect and touch and greet each other."

Rainer Maria Rilke

"To love oneself is the beginning of a lifelong romance."

Oscar Wilde

"Love is when you meet someone who tells you something new about yourself."

Andre Breton

"Love is the word used to label the sexual excitement of the young, the habituation of the middle-aged, and the mutual dependence of the old."

John Ciardi

"It is easier to love humanity as a whole than to love one's neighbor."

Eric Hoffer

"Love is a serious mental disease."

Plato

Pleasure

"A pleasure is not full grown
until it is remembered."

C. S. Lewis

"Do not bite at the bait of pleasure till you know there is no hook beneath it."

Thomas Jefferson

"Perhaps all pleasure is only relief."

William S. Burroughs

"The essence of pleasure is spontaneity."

Germaine Greer

"Most men pursue pleasure with such breathless haste that they hurry past it."

Soren Kierkegaard

"A cigarette is the perfect type of a perfect pleasure. It is exquisite, and it leaves one unsatisfied. What more can one want?"

Oscar Wilde

"There is no pleasure in having nothing to do; the fun is in having lots to do and not doing it."

Mary Wilson Little

"A life of pleasure makes even the strongest mind frivolous at last."

Edward G. Bulwer Lytton

"The test and the use of man's education is that he finds pleasure in the exercise of his mind."

Jacques Barzun

"Short is the joy that guilty pleasure brings."

Euripides

"What we call pleasure, and rightly so, is the absence of all pain."

Cicero

"Pleasure is an important component of the quality of life, but by itself it does not bring happiness."

Mihaly Csikszentmihalyi

"The aim of the wise is not to secure pleasure, but to avoid pain."

Aristotle

"I believe that every human mind feels pleasure in doing good to another."

Thomas Jefferson

"The noblest pleasure is the joy of understanding."

Leonardo da Vinci

"There is no such thing as pure pleasure, some anxiety always goes with it."

Ovid

"Man is not constituted to take pleasure in the same things always."

Sophocles

"Pleasure and pain, though directly opposite are contrived to be constant companions."

Pierre Charron

Pride

"Pride is the mask we make of our faults."

Hebrew Proverb

"Pride is a powerful narcotic, but it doesn't do much for the auto-immune system."

Stuart Stevens

"Pride is an admission of weakness, it secretly fears all competition and dreads all rivals."

Fulton J. Sheen

"Memory says: I did that. Pride replies: I could not have done that. Eventually memory yields."

Friedrich Nietzsche

"Pride is the recognition of the fact that you are your own highest value and, like all of man's values, it has to be earned."

Ayn Rand

"Pride is a spiritual Cancer: it eats up the very possibility of love, or contentment, or even common sense."

C. S. Lewis

"Humility is the ability to give up your pride and still retain your dignity."

Vanna Bonta

"It was pride that changed angels into devils."

Saint Augustine

"Pride makes us artificial and humility makes us real."

Thomas Merton

"If I had only one sermon to preach it would be a sermon against pride."

Gilbert K. Chesterton

"Is pride, the never-failing vice of fools."

Alexander Pope

"It is not the broken heart that kills, but broken pride."

Gilbert Parker

"Pride is the first step in people unraveling and companies unraveling and relationships unraveling."

Jeff Foxworthy

"What is pride? A rocket that emulates the stars."

William Wordsworth

Regret

"Regret for wasted time
is more wasted time."

Mason Cooley

"Regret for the things we did can be tempered by time; it is regret for the things we did not do that is inconsolable."

Sidney J. Harris

"Never regret. If it's good, it's wonderful. If it's bad, it's experience."

Victoria Holt

"The only thing I regret about my past is the length of it. If I had to live my life again I'd make all the same mistakes, only sooner."

Tallulah Bankhead

"It took me less than half a lifetime to realize that regret is one of the few guaranteed certainties. Sooner or later everything is touched by it, despite our naive and senseless hope that just this time we will be spared its cold hand on our heart."

Jonathan Carroll

"Never regret something that once made you smile."

Amber Deckers

"I never regret anything. Because every little detail of your life is what made you into who you are in the end."

Drew Barrymore

"The regrets of yesterday and the fear of tomorrow can kill you."

Liza Minelli

"I have a lot of regrets, but I'm not going to think of them as regrets."

Debbie Harry

"Let us not bankrupt our todays by paying interest on the regrets of yesterday and by borrowing in advance the troubles of tomorrow."

Ralph W. Sockman

"A man is not old until regrets take the place of dreams."

John Barrymore

"I think it's very good to have regrets, to learn how to live with them."

Keren Ann

"We should regret our mistakes and learn from them, but never carry them forward into the future with us."

Lucy Maud Montgomery

Sadness

"Sadness is but a wall
between two gardens."

Khalil Gibran

"The word "happiness" would lose its meaning if it were not balanced by sadness."

Carl Jung

"Sad are only those who understand."

Arab Proverb

"We never taste happiness in perfection, our most fortunate successes are mixed with sadness."

Pierre Corneille

"Sadness flies away on the wings of time."

Jean de La Fontaine

"All pleasures contain an element of sadness."

Jonathan Eibeschutz

"In depression you care about nothing. In sadness you care about everything."

Gloria Steinem

"One must not let oneself be overwhelmed by sadness."

Jackie Kennedy

"In deep sadness there is no place for sentimentality."

William S. Burroughs

"Experiencing sadness and anger can make you feel more creative, and by being creative, you can get beyond your pain or negativity."

Yoko Ono

"Sadness is also a kind of defence."

Ivo Andric

"I do believe that if you haven't learnt about sadness, you cannot appreciate happiness."

Nana Mouskouri

Shame

"The only shame is to have none."

Blaise Pascal

"We all have thoughts that would shame the devil."
Mark Twain

"Where the mind is past hope, the heart is past shame."
John Lyly

"Doubt is the brother of shame."
Erik Erikson

"Whatever is begun in anger, ends in shame."
Benjamin Franklin

"Shame is such an intense emotion. It just can drive you."
Kyra Sedgwick

"I gave up shame a long time ago."
John Lithgow

"Shame may restrain what law does not prohibit."
Lucius Annaeus Seneca

"There is no shame in not knowing, the shame lies in not finding out."
Russian proverb

Enjoy other **little BIG Books** titles at fine ebook retailers everywhere.

www.facebook.com/littlebigbooks2

littlebigbooks@icloud.com

www.ingramcontent.com/pod-product-compliance
Lightning Source LLC
Chambersburg PA
CBHW070536290526
45790CB00002B/520